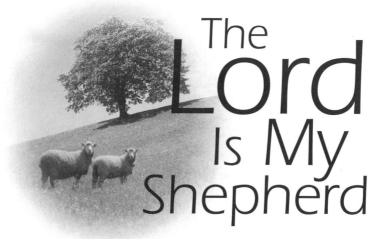

The Lord Is My Shepherd

Discovery Series Bible Study

The sight of sheep grazing peacefully on a grassy hillside brings a sense of well-being to even the most troubled heart. Perhaps it is because of the symbolism the image carries—helpless, defenseless creatures able to munch contentedly under the watchful eye of one they have learned to trust.

Jesus called His followers sheep, and as His sheep we long to comprehend what it means to find contentment under the watchful eye of our loving, trustworthy, heavenly Shepherd.

In this excerpt of *Psalm 23: The Song Of A Passionate Heart*, author David Roper examines the first two verses of this well-known psalm. He looks at the importance of the shepherd metaphor throughout Scripture and then gives practical help in experiencing the rest that our Shepherd has prepared for us.

Martin R. De Haan II, President of RBC Ministries

Publisher: Discovery House Publishers
Editor: David Sper
Graphic Design: Alex Soh, Janet Chim, Ineke K.
Cover Photo: Alex Soh © 2001 RBC Ministries Asia Ltd.
Illustrations: Stan D. Myers, Ineke K.
Series Coordinator / Study Guide: Bill Crowder, Sim Kay Tee

This *Discovery Series Bible Study* is based on *The Lord Is My Shepherd* (HP952), one of the popular *Discovery Series* booklets from RBC Ministries. With more than 140 titles on a variety of biblical and Christian-living issues, these 32-page booklets offer a rich resource of insight for your study of God's Word.
For a catalog of *Discovery Series* booklets, write to us at:
RBC Ministries, PO Box 2222, Grand Rapids, MI 49501-2222
Or, visit us on the Web at: www.discoveryseries.org

Discovery House Publishers

A member of the RBC Ministries family:
Our Daily Bread, Day Of Discovery, RBC Radio, Discovery Series, Campus Journal, Discovery House Music, Sports Spectrum

ISBN 1-57293-097-7

Table Of Contents

A Portrait Of God

The problem with most of us is that we have no clear picture of the God we long to worship. Our image of Him is clouded by the memory of cold cathedrals and bitter religions, by pastors or priests who put the fear of God into us, or by all that we suffered as children from fathers who were absent, emotionally detached, brutal, or weak. All of us have inexact notions of God.

> **The problem with most of us is that**
> **we have no clear picture of the God we long to worship.**

So the question is God Himself: Who is He? This is the question to which all others lead—the question that God Himself put into our hearts. (And if He put it into our hearts, there must be an answer in His heart waiting to be revealed.)

David gave us a comforting and compelling answer: "The Lord is my shepherd" (Ps. 23:1).

"Yahweh is my shepherd" is what David actually wrote, using the name that God gave Himself. An older generation of scholars referred to the name as the "Ineffable Tetragrammaton"—the unutterable four-letter word. The letters that make up God's name (written without vowels as YHWH) were rarely pronounced by the Jews for fear of arousing God's wrath. Instead, they substituted some lesser word like *Adonai* (my Lord) or *Elohim* (the generic name for God).

The term *Yahweh*, sometimes shortened to *Yah* in the Old Testament, comes from a form of the Hebrew verb "to be." This suggests that God is a self-sufficient God. But that explanation is cold comfort to me. I prefer David's description: "Yahweh is my shepherd."

Shepherd is a modest metaphor, yet one that is loaded with meaning. Part of the comparison is the portrayal of a shepherd and his sheep; the other is David's experience and ours. David painted a picture and put us into it. The genius of the psalm is that it belongs to us. We can use David's words as our own.

**David painted a picture and put us into it.
The genius of the psalm is that it belongs to us.**

David's opening statement, "The Lord is my shepherd," introduces the controlling image that appears throughout the poem. Each line elaborates the symbol, filling out the picture, showing us how our Shepherd-God leads us to that place where we shall no longer want.

David And The Shepherd Metaphor

David himself was a shepherd. He spent much of his youth tending his "few sheep in the desert" (1 Sam. 17:28). The desert is one of the best places in the world to learn. There are few distractions and there is little that can be used. In such a place we're more inclined to think about the meaning of things than about what those things provide.

One day as David was watching his sheep, the idea came to him that God was like a shepherd. He thought of the incessant care that sheep require—their helplessness and defenselessness. He recalled their foolish straying from safe paths and their constant need for a guide. He thought of the time and patience it took for them to trust him before they would follow. He remembered the times when he led them through danger and they huddled close at his heels. He pondered the fact that he must think for his sheep, fight for them, guard them, and find their pasture and quiet pools. He remembered their bruises and scratches that he bound up, and he marveled at how frequently he had to rescue them from harm. Yet not one of his sheep was aware of how well it was watched. Yes, he mused, God is very much like a good shepherd.

> **David marveled at how frequently he had to rescue his sheep from harm. Yet not one of them was aware of how well it was watched.**

Ancient shepherds knew their sheep by name. They were acquainted with all their ways—their peculiarities, their characteristic marks, their tendencies, their idiosyncrasies.

6

Back then, shepherds didn't drive their sheep; they led them. At the shepherd's morning call—a distinctive guttural sound—each flock would rise and follow its master to the feeding grounds. Even if two shepherds called their flocks at the same time and the sheep were intermingled, they never followed the wrong shepherd. All day long the sheep followed their own shepherd as he searched the wilderness looking for grassy meadows and sheltered pools where his flock could feed and drink in peace.

At certain times of the year, it became necessary to move the flocks deeper into the wilderness, a desolate wasteland where predators lurked. But the sheep were always well-guarded. Shepherds carried a "rod" (a heavy club) on their belts and a shepherd's staff in their hands. The staff had a crook that was used to extricate the sheep from perilous places or to restrain them from wandering away. The club was a weapon to ward off beasts. David said, "When a lion or a bear came and carried off a sheep from the flock, I went after it, struck it, and rescued the sheep from its mouth" (1 Sam. 17:34-35).

**A good shepherd never left his sheep alone.
They would have been lost without him.
His presence was their assurance.**

Throughout the day each shepherd stayed close to his sheep, watching them carefully and protecting them from the slightest harm. When one sheep strayed, the shepherd searched for it until it was found. Then he laid it across his shoulders and brought it back home. At the end of the day, each shepherd led his flock to the safety of the fold and slept across the gateway to protect them.

A good shepherd never left his sheep alone. They would have been lost without him. His presence was their assurance.

It's this good shepherd that David envisioned as he composed each line of Psalm 23.

A Portrait Of God; David & The Shepherd Metaphor

Psalm 23:1—"The Lord is my shepherd; I shall not want."

Objective:
To understand how David modeled the picture of a shepherd.

Bible Memorization:
Psalm 23:1

Read:
"A Portrait Of God"; "David & The Shepherd Metaphor"
pp.4-7

Warming Up
Why do you think many people consider Psalm 23 their favorite Bible passage? Is Psalm 23 one of your favorite texts? Why or why not?

Thinking Through
On page 4 we read, "All of us have inexact notions of God." What does the author mean by that? What are some "inexact notions" you have had of God? Why is it important that we correct our "inexact notions"?

David's answer to the question "Who is God?" was to respond, "The Lord is my shepherd." Why is the word *shepherd* such an apt metaphor for God's work in our lives? (see pp.4-5).

How did David see God's care for His people paralleled in a shepherd's care for his flock? (see pp.6-7).

Digging In
Key Text: Psalm 23:1
In verse 1, David used the four-letter Hebrew word *YHWH* (Jehovah, which is translated "Lord" in our English Bibles) to refer to God. What does this tell you about the kind of shepherd God is?

What did David mean when he said, "I shall not want"? Why was he able to say that in the context of the Lord as his shepherd? What are some of the "wants" that David may have been referring to?

How do David's words carry a tone of confidence in God's trustworthiness? Was his confidence justified? Is it a confidence that you are able to share? Why or why not?

Going Further
Refer
What are some ways that the Lord's shepherding care is seen in David's care for his own sheep in 1 Samuel 17:34-35?

"The Lord is my shepherd; I shall not want."
Psalm 23:1

Reflect
Consider David's statement, "The Lord is my shepherd." Are you comfortable making this declaration of dependence and trust? In what ways have you experienced the reality that God is your shepherd?

In light of the circumstances and needs in your life at this moment, are you able say that you "shall not want"? Why or why not?

A PORTRAIT OF GOD (PART 2)

Others
Who Used The
Shepherd
Metaphor

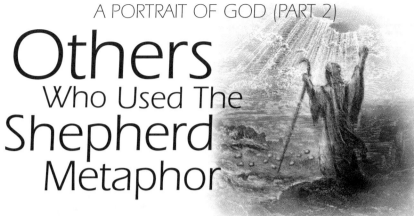

JACOB: GOD ACCEPTS US

The patriarch Jacob was a shepherd and the first person in the Bible to make use of the shepherd metaphor for God. As he lay dying, he looked back over his life and summed it up with these words: "God . . . has been my shepherd all my life to this day" (Gen. 48:15).

Jacob was born with a difficult disposition. Gripping his twin brother's heel at birth, he continued throughout his life to try to trip him up and get ahead of him. In fact, Jacob's whole life was characterized by wheeling, double-dealing, grasping, grabbing, and jerking people around to gain selfish advantage. Yet God was not ashamed to be called "the God of Jacob" and to be his shepherd every day of his life.

Jacob is reminiscent of those who come into life with a pervasive tendency to go wrong. They inhabit inherited hells—saddled from birth with insecurities, insanities, and sinful predilections. They are addicted to food, sex, alcohol, drugs, spending, gambling, or working. They have disturbed and difficult personalities, and have, as C. S. Lewis said, a "hard machine to drive."

God knows our tiresome stories. He understands the latent forces and all the sources and possibilities of evil in our natures. He sees the hurt and the heartbreak that others cannot see and that cannot be explained, even to our closest friends. He's aware of the reasons for our moodiness, our temper tantrums, our selfish indulgences. Others may be put off by our disposition, but God never turns away. He sees beyond the prickliness to the broken heart. His understanding is infinite.

How damaged we are or how far wrong we've gone doesn't make a difference to Him. Our vileness does not alter His character. He is eternal love—the same yesterday, today, forever. We are not what He wants us to be, but we are not unwanted. If we will have Him, He will be our shepherd.

Fredrick Buechner marvels at the folly of God to welcome "lamebrains and misfits and nit-pickers and holier-than-thous and stuffed shirts and odd ducks and egomaniacs and milquetoasts and closet sensualists," but that's the way He is. Whatever we are, wherever we are, His heart is open to us.

ISAIAH: GOD KNOWS US INTIMATELY

Isaiah envisioned a stellar Shepherd who each night called out His star-flock by name:

> Lift your eyes and look to the heavens: Who created all these? He who brings out the starry host one by one, and calls them each by name. Because of His great power and mighty strength, not one of them is missing (Isa. 40:26).

It's not by chance that the stars have their assigned orbits and places in the universe. They do not rise at random, nor do they wander haphazardly through space. They rise at God's beck and call. He brings out the starry host one by one and calls them each by name. Not one is forgotten. Not one is overlooked. Not one is left behind.

It's a terrible thing to be unknown. We live in fear that we will never be known enough—that others will never know who we really are, what our dreams are, and where our thoughts are taking us. Yet we have nothing to fear. God knows every one of His sheep by name.

He's aware of each personality and peculiarity. There are the little ones that have to be carried, the cripples that can't keep up, the nursing ewes that won't be hurried, the old sheep that can barely get along. There are the bellwethers that always want to be out front, the bullies that butt and push to get their way, the timid ones (the sheepish) that are afraid to follow, the black sheep that are always the exception. There are those who graze their way into lostness and others more deliberately on the lam. The Good Shepherd knows us all.

The Sovereign Lord comes with power, and His arm rules for Him. . . .
He tends His flock like a shepherd: He gathers the lambs in His arms and
carries them close to His heart; He gently leads those that have young
(Isa. 40:10-11).

God knows our pace. He knows when grief, pain, and loneliness overwhelm us. He knows when the full realization of our limitations comes home to us. He knows when we're shamed and broken and unable to go on. God does not drive His sheep, He gently leads them. He allows for hesitation and trepidation. He gives credit for decisions and resolutions that are strenuously tested. He understands courage that falters in the face of terrible odds. He can accommodate a faith that flames out under stress. He takes into account the hidden reasons for failure. He feels the full weight of our disasters. He knows our pain as no one else knows it. Our bleating reaches His ears. He even hears our inarticulate cries.

When we lag behind, He does not scold us. Rather, He gathers us up, encircles us with His strong arm, and carries us next to His heart. The essence, the central core of God's character, lies here: He has the heart of a tender shepherd.

JEREMIAH: GOD PURSUES US IN LOVE

The prophet Jeremiah saw a flock of ruined sheep:

My people have been lost [ruined] sheep; their shepherds have led them
astray and caused them to roam on the mountains. They wandered over
mountain and hill and forgot their own resting place. . . . But I will bring
Israel back to his own pasture (Jer. 50:6,19).

We readily forget God, our "resting place," and wander away. Yet He pursues us wherever we go, with no complaint of the darkness, the cold wind, the heavy burden, the steep hill, or the thorny path over which He must pass to rescue one lost sheep. His love does not count time, energy, suffering, or even life itself.

His pursuit is not a reward for our goodness but the result of His decision to love. He is driven by love, not by our beauty. He is drawn to us when we have done nothing right and when we have done everything wrong. Jesus said:

What do you think? If a man owns a hundred sheep, and one of them wanders away, will he not leave the ninety-nine on the hills and go to look for the one that wandered off? And if he finds it, I tell you the truth, he is happier about that one sheep than about the ninety-nine that did not wander off. In the same way your Father in heaven is not willing that any of these little ones should be lost (Mt. 18:12-14).

Lost sheep are not doomed. They're the ones He came to find.

EZEKIEL: GOD TENDERLY CARES FOR US

Ezekiel announced the birth of that best of all shepherds long before He was born. He said that when He came He would tend God's flock with tender, loving care:

My sheep wandered over all the mountains and on every high hill. They were scattered over the whole earth, and no one searched or looked for them. . . . For this is what the Sovereign Lord says: "I Myself will search for My sheep and look after them. As a shepherd looks after his scattered flock when he is with them, so will I look after My sheep. I will rescue them from all the places where they were scattered on a day of clouds and darkness. . . . I will tend them in a good pasture . . . . There they will lie down in good grazing land, and there they will feed in a rich pasture . . . . I Myself will tend My sheep and have them lie down," declares the Sovereign Lord. "I will search for the lost and bring back the strays. I will bind up the injured and strengthen the weak" (Ezek. 34:6,11-12,14-16).

It was Ezekiel's task to care for scattered exiles far from home. He described them as sheep that were scattered "because there was no shepherd . . . . and no one searched or looked for them" (vv.5-6).

Israel's disbanding was their own fault, the result of years of resistance to God. They had looked to their idols and shed blood, and they had defiled their neighbors' wives and done other detestable things (Ezek. 33:25-26). That's why they were estranged. Yet God said, "I will search for the lost and bring back the strays" (34:16). Good shepherds don't look *down* on lost sheep; they look *for* them.

Sheep don't have to go looking for their shepherd—it's the other way around. He's out looking for them. Even if the sheep aren't thinking about the Shepherd, He pursues them to the ends of the earth. Simon Tugwell wrote, "He follows them into their own long, dark, journey; there, where they thought finally to escape Him, they run straight into His arms."

There is, in fact, no way to escape Him except by running into His arms. Though we are stiff-necked and stubborn, He is equally stiff-necked and stubborn. He will never give up His pursuit. He cannot get us off of His mind.

Furthermore, Ezekiel said, when the Good Shepherd finds His sheep He looks after them: "As a shepherd looks after his scattered flock when he is with them, so will I look after My sheep" (34:12). "Look after" suggests careful examination of each animal. Our Shepherd-God is a good shepherd. He knows well the condition of His flock. He sees the marks of sorrow on each face. He knows every cut and bruise, every ache and pain. He recognizes the signs of hounding, misuse, and abuse—the wounds that others have given us and the residue of our own resistance.

He promises to do what other shepherds cannot or will not do: "I will bind up the injured and strengthen the weak" (34:16). He has compassion on the afflicted and the handicapped, on those wounded by their own sin. He understands sorrow, misfortune, broken homes, shattered ambition. "He heals the brokenhearted and binds up their wounds" (Ps. 147:3). He applies the balm that makes the wounded whole. That's the comfort of God to our beleaguered hearts.

But there is more. Another Good Shepherd was on the way—One who would be one with the Father in pastoral compassion:

> I will place over them one [unique] shepherd, My servant David, and he
> will tend them; he will tend them and be their shepherd. I the Lord will
> be their God, and My servant David will be prince among them. I the
> Lord have spoken (Ezek. 34:23-24).

God was speaking of David's long-awaited Son, our Lord Jesus, that Great Shepherd who lays down His life for the sheep (Jn. 10:11).

⊗

STUDY
NO. **2**

Others And The Shepherd Metaphor

Isaiah 40:11—"He will feed His flock like a shepherd; He will gather the lambs with His arm, and carry them in His bosom, and gently lead those who are with young."

Objective:

To see how the Old Testament uses the shepherd metaphor to describe God's care for His children.

Bible Memorization:
Isaiah 40:11

Read:
"Others Who Used The Shepherd Metaphor" pp.11-15

Warming Up
The Bible repeatedly uses the image of sheep to describe people. In what ways are we similar to sheep?

Thinking Through
In this section, we see how Jacob, Isaiah, Jeremiah, and Ezekiel used the shepherd metaphor to demonstrate four elements of God's concern for His people. What are those four things?

Of the four expressions of God's concern seen in answer to the previous question, which one is the most meaningful to you at this point in your life? Why?

How does the phrase "look after" (see p.15) describe the care of our Shepherd for His sheep? How have you seen those indications of care reflected in your own experience?

Digging In
Key Text: Ezekiel 34:11-12,14-16
Various groups of sheep are mentioned in Ezekiel 34:14-16. What are they? How do they represent various groups of people?

What kind of care does each of these groups of sheep need? In this passage, what did God say that He Himself would do for each of these kinds of sheep?

In verse 16, there are expressions of mercy followed by expressions of judgment. Why are the statements of judgment there, and why do you think the "fat and the strong" will be judged?

Going Further
Refer
In Ezekiel 34:23-24, what is God's promise to His flock? Who is this promised Shepherd and why is it important?

Reflect
On page 14 we read, "Lost sheep are not doomed. They're the ones He came to find." Describe how the Good Shepherd came looking for you and found you.

In your opinion, what kind of a sheep are you: protected, well-fed, satisfied, fat, restless, wandering, rebellious, lost, hungry, injured, tired, weak, dying, forgotten? Why? How does God care for sheep like you?

11 "For thus says the Lord God: 'Indeed I Myself will search for My sheep and seek them out. 12 As a shepherd seeks out his flock on the day he is among his scattered sheep, so will I seek out My sheep and deliver them from all the places where they were scattered on a cloudy and dark day.'"
Ezekiel 34:11-12

14 "'I will feed them in good pasture, and their fold shall be on the high mountains of Israel. There they shall lie down in a good fold and feed in rich pasture on the mountains of Israel. 15 I will feed My flock, and I will make them lie down,' says the Lord God. 16 'I will seek what was lost and bring back what was driven away, bind up the broken and strengthen what was sick; but I will destroy the fat and the strong, and feed them in judgment.'"
Ezekiel 34:14-16

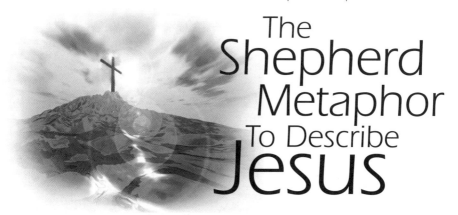

The Shepherd Metaphor To Describe Jesus

Some 600 years after David composed his Shepherd Song, Jesus said with quiet assurance:

> *I am the good shepherd. The good shepherd lays down His life for the sheep. The hired hand is not the shepherd who owns the sheep. So when he sees the wolf coming, he abandons the sheep and runs away. Then the wolf attacks the flock and scatters it. The man runs away because he is a hired hand and cares nothing for the sheep. I am the good shepherd; I know My sheep and My sheep know Me—just as the Father knows Me and I know the Father—and I lay down My life for the sheep (Jn. 10:11-15).*

This is our Lord Jesus, "that great Shepherd of the sheep" (Heb. 13:20). He was one with the Father. He too saw us as "sheep without a shepherd." He "came to seek and to save what was lost" (Lk. 19:10). He's the one who left the "ninety-nine on the hills" and went "to look for the one that wandered away," forever establishing the value of one person and the Father's desire that not one of them should perish (Mt. 18:12-14).

F. B. Meyer wrote, "He has a shepherd's *heart*, beating with pure and generous love that counted not His own life-blood too dear a price to pay down as our ransom. He has a shepherd's *eye*, that takes in the whole flock and misses not even the poor sheep wandering away on the mountains cold. He has a shepherd's *faithfulness*, which will never fail or forsake, leave us comfortless, nor flee when He sees the wolf coming. He has a shepherd's *strength*, so that He is well able to deliver us from the jaw of the lion or the paw of the bear. He has a shepherd's *tenderness*; no lamb so tiny that He will not carry it; no saint so weak that He will not gently lead; no soul so faint that He will not give it rest. . . . His gentleness makes great."

But there's more: The Good Shepherd laid down His life for the sheep. Since the beginning of time, religions have decreed that a lamb should give up its life for the shepherd. The shepherd would bring his lamb to the sanctuary, lean with all his weight on the lamb's head, and confess his sin. The lamb would be slain and its blood would flow out—a life for a life.

What irony! Now the Shepherd gives up His life for His lamb. "He was pierced for our transgressions, He was crushed for our iniquities; the punishment that brought us peace was upon Him, and by His wounds we are healed. We all, like sheep, have gone astray, each of us has turned to his own way; and the Lord has laid on Him the iniquity of us all" (Isa. 53:5-6).

The story is about the death of the Shepherd. "He Himself bore our sins in His body on the tree, so that we might die to sins and live for righteousness; by His wounds you have been healed" (1 Pet. 2:24). He died for *all* sin—the obvious sins of murder, adultery, and theft as well as for the secret sins of selfishness and pride. He Himself bore our sins in His body on the cross. This was sin's final cure.

The normal way of looking at the cross is to say that man was so bad and God was so mad that someone had to pay. But it was not anger that led Christ to be crucified; it was love. The crucifixion is the point of the story. God loves us so much that He Himself took on our guilt. He internalized all our sin and healed it. When it was over He said, "It is finished!" There is nothing left for us to do but to enter into forgiving acceptance—and for those of us who have already entered it, to enter into more of it.

The Shepherd calls to us and listens for the slightest sounds of life. He hears the faintest cry. If He hears nothing at all, He will not give up or go away. He lets us wander away, hoping that weariness and despair will turn us around.

Our discomfort is God's doing. He hounds us. He hems us in. He thwarts our dreams. He foils our best-laid plans. He frustrates our hopes. He waits until we know that nothing will ease our pain, nothing will make life worth living except His presence. And when we turn to Him, He is there to greet us. He has been there all along. "The Lord is near to all who call on Him" (Ps. 145:18).

But, you say, "Why would He want me? He knows my sin, my wandering, my long habits of yielding. I'm not good enough. I'm not sorry enough for my sin. I'm unable not to sin."

Our waywardness doesn't have to be explained to God. He's never surprised by anything we do. He sees everything at a single glance—what is, what could have been, what would have been apart from our sinful choices. He sees into the dark corners and crannies of our hearts and knows everything about us there is to know. But what He sees only draws out His love. There is no deeper motivation in God than love. It is His nature to love; He can do no other, for "God is love" (1 Jn. 4:8).

Do you have some nameless grief? Some vague, sad pain? Some inexplicable ache in your heart? Come to Him who made your heart. Jesus said, "Come to Me, all you who are weary and burdened, and I will give you rest. Take My yoke upon you and learn from Me, for I am gentle and humble in heart, and you will find rest for your souls. For My yoke is easy and My burden is light" (Mt. 11:28-30).

To know that God is like this and to know this God is rest. There is no more profound lesson than this: He is the one thing that we need.

The word *shepherd* carries with it thoughts of tenderness, security, and provision, yet it means nothing as long as I cannot say, "The Lord is *my* shepherd."

What a difference that monosyllable makes—all the difference in the world. It means that I can have all of God's attention, all of the time, just as though I'm the only one. I may be part of a flock, but I'm one of a kind.

It's one thing to say, "The Lord is *a* shepherd." It's another to say, "The Lord is *my* shepherd." Martin Luther observed that faith is a matter of personal pronouns: *My* Lord and *my* God. This is the faith that saves.

The Shepherd Metaphor And Jesus

Isaiah 53:6—"All we like sheep have gone astray; we have turned, every one, to his own way; and the Lord has laid on Him the iniquity of us all."

Objective:

To see and embrace Jesus as the Good Shepherd.

Bible Memorization:

Isaiah 53:6

Read:

"The Shepherd Metaphor To Describe Jesus" pp.19-21

Warming Up

In the parable of the lost sheep (Mt. 18:12-14), the shepherd left 99 sheep in the fold and pursued the one that was lost. Can you remember times when you were the lost sheep Jesus pursued? What was it like when you were back in the fold?

Thinking Through

F. B. Meyer is quoted on pages 19-20 as naming five characteristics of Jesus as the Good Shepherd. What are they, and which is the most comforting to you? Why?

According to page 20, why is it ironic that the Good Shepherd sacrificed Himself for His sheep? Why was His sacrifice necessary and what did it accomplish?

A key thought on page 21 is the need to call Jesus *our* shepherd, not just *a* shepherd. Why did Luther describe the difference between those two ideas as "the faith that saves"?

Digging In
Key Text: John 10:11-16

What distinguishes the hireling from the shepherd in this passage? Why would the good shepherd lay down his life for his sheep? (see vv.11,15).

What distinguishes his flock from other flocks? How would his sheep know him? Who are the other sheep the shepherd must bring into his fold? How is this accomplished?

What does Christ mean in verse 16 when He says, "There will be one flock and one shepherd"?

Going Further
Refer
In Matthew 18:12-14, why did the shepherd leave the 99 sheep to search for the one that was lost? Why would he "rejoice more" over finding that one lost sheep than over the ones who remained?

Reflect
Are you prone to drift from Christ? Why? When you felt like the one sheep that had wandered off, how did the Good Shepherd bring you back into His care?

Keeping in mind the Shepherd's attitude toward wandering sheep and our own tendency to drift, what should be our response to others who have gone astray? Support your answer with Scripture.

[11]"I am the good shepherd. The good shepherd gives His life for the sheep. [12]But a hireling, he who is not the shepherd, one who does not own the sheep, sees the wolf coming and leaves the sheep and flees; and the wolf catches the sheep and scatters them. [13]The hireling flees because he is a hireling and does not care about the sheep. [14]I am the good shepherd; and I know My sheep, and am known by My own. [15]As the Father knows Me, even so I know the Father; and I lay down My life for the sheep. [16]And other sheep I have which are not of this fold; them also I must bring, and they will hear My voice; and there will be one flock and one shepherd."
John 10:11-16

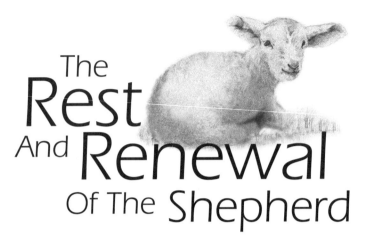

The Rest And Renewal Of The Shepherd

Left to ourselves we would have nothing more than restlessness, driven by the realization that there is something more to know and love. But God will not leave us to ourselves. According to Psalm 23:2, He *makes* us lie down in green pastures He *leads* us beside quiet waters. The verbs suggest gentle persuasion—a shepherd patiently, persistently encouraging his sheep to the place where their hungers and thirsts will be assuaged.

In David's day, "green pastures" were oases, verdant places in the desert toward which shepherds led their thirsty flocks. Left to themselves, sheep would wander off into the wilderness and die. Experienced shepherds knew the terrain and urged their flocks toward familiar grasslands and streams where they could forage and feed, lie down and rest.

The picture here is not of sheep grazing and drinking, but at rest, lying down—"stretched out" to use David's word. The verb *leads* suggests a slow and leisurely pace. The scene is one of tranquility, satisfaction, and rest.

The common practice of shepherds was to graze their flocks in rough pasture early in the morning, leading them to better grasses as the morning progressed, and then coming to a cool and shaded oasis for noontime rest.

The image of placid waters emphasizes the concept of rest—the condition of having all our passions satisfied. Augustine cried out, "What will make me take my rest in You . . . so I can forget my restlessness and take hold of You, the one good thing in my life?"

The compulsion begins with God. "He makes me [causes me to] lie down in green pastures, He leads me beside quiet waters" (23:2). The Good Shepherd "calls his own sheep by name and leads them out. When he has brought out all his own, he goes on ahead of them, and his sheep follow him because they know his voice" (Jn. 10:3-4).

God makes the first move. He takes the initiative by calling us and leading us to a place of rest. It's not because we're seeking God; He is seeking us.

God's cry to wayward Adam and Eve, "Where are you?" suggests the loneliness He feels when separated from those He loves. G. K. Chesterton suggests that the whole Bible is about the "loneliness of God." I like the thought that in some inexplicable way God misses me; that He can't bear to be separated from me; that I'm always on His mind; that He patiently, insistently calls me and seeks me, not for my own sake alone, but for His. He cries, "Where are you?"

> **God makes the first move.**
> **He takes the initiative by calling us and**
> **leading us to a place of rest.**

Deep within us is a place for God. We were made for God and without His love we ache in loneliness and emptiness. He calls from deep space to our depths: "Deep calls to deep" (Ps. 42:7).

David put it this way, "My heart says of You, 'Seek His face!' 'Your face, Lord, I will seek'" (Ps. 27:8). God spoke to the depths of David's heart, uttering His heart's desire: "Seek My face." And David responded with alacrity, "I will seek Your face, Lord."

And so it is: God calls us—seeking us to seek Him—and our hearts resonate with longing for Him. That understanding has radically changed the way I look at my relationship to God. It is now neither duty nor discipline—a regimen I impose on myself like 100 sit-ups and 50 push-ups each day—but a response, an answer, to One who has been calling me all my life.

What are those green pastures and quiet waters to which God leads us?

Where are they? What is the reality behind these metaphors?

God Himself is our "true pasture" (Jer. 50:7) and our pool of quiet water. He is our true nourishment, our living water. If we do not take Him in, we will starve.

> **There is a hunger in the human heart which nothing but God can satisfy. There is a thirst that no one but He can quench.**

There is a hunger in the human heart which nothing but God can satisfy. There is a thirst that no one but He can quench. "Do not work for food that spoils," Jesus said, "but for food that endures to eternal life, which the Son of Man will give you. . . . I am the bread of life. He who comes to Me will never go hungry, and he who believes in Me will never be thirsty" (Jn. 6:27,35).

Malcolm Muggeridge's confession is a striking expression of this thought:

I may, I suppose, regard myself as being a relatively successful man. People occasionally look at me on the street. That's *fame*. I can fairly easily earn enough to qualify for the highest slopes of inland revenue. That's *success*. Furnished with money and a little fame, even the elderly, if they care to, can partake of trendy diversions. That's *pleasure*. It might happen once in a while that something I said or wrote was sufficiently heeded to persuade myself that it represented a serious impact on our time. That's *fulfillment*. Yet I say to you, and I beg of you to believe me, multiply these tiny triumphs by a million, add them all together, and they are nothing, less than nothing, a positive impediment, measured against one draught of that living water that is offered to the spiritually hungry.

But how do we "graze" on God and "drink" Him in?

Once more we're confronted with symbolism. What do the metaphors mean?

The process begins, as all relationships do, with a "meeting." As David said:

As the deer pants for streams of water, so my soul pants for You, O God. My soul thirsts for God, for the living God. When can I go and meet with God? (Ps. 42:1-2).

God is a real person. He is not a human invention, a concept, a theory, or a projection of ourselves. He is overwhelmingly alive—real beyond our wildest dreams. He can be "met" to use David's commonplace word. A. W. Tozer wrote:

God is a Person and as such can be cultivated as any person can. God is a Person and in the depths of His mighty nature He thinks, wills, enjoys, feels, loves, desires, and suffers as any other person may. God is a Person and can be known in increasing degrees of intimacy as we prepare our hearts for the wonder of it.

That's the reality, but it's also the rub: Are we willing to prepare ourselves to meet Him? He responds to the slightest approach, but we're only as close as we want to be. "If . . . you seek the Lord your God, you will find Him," Moses promised, then added this proviso: "if you look for Him with all your heart and with all your soul" (Dt. 4:29).

We don't have to look very hard or very long for God. He's only as far away as our hearts (Rom. 10:8-9), but He will not intrude. He calls us, but then waits for our answer. Our progress toward Him is determined by our desire to engage Him in a personal way—to know Him.

> **God is only as far away as our hearts, but He will not intrude.**

We say, "Something's wrong with me. I'm not happy. There must be something more," but we do nothing about our discontent. It's this mood of resignation that keeps us from joy. Our first task is to get honest with ourselves. Do we want God or not? If we do, we must be willing to make the effort to respond to Him. "Come near to God," said James, "and He will come near to you" (Jas. 4:8). It's a matter of desire. "O God, You are my God, earnestly I seek You," the psalmist said (Ps. 63:1).

Taking Time Alone With God

"Begin small and start promptly" is an old Quaker saying. The idea is to keep things simple and to begin soon. Simplicity begins with solitude—not mere time alone, but time alone with God.

Henri Nouwen wrote, "Solitude begins with a time and place for God, and Him alone. If we really believe not only that God exists, but that He is actively present in our lives—healing, teaching, and guiding—we need to set aside a time and space to give Him our undivided attention."

But where can we find that solitude? Where can we find a quiet place in the midst of the din and demands of this world? "In a crowd, it's difficult to see God," Augustine said. "This vision craves secret retirement." "Go into your room," Jesus said, "close the door and pray to your Father, who is unseen" (Mt. 6:6).

**Solitude is a healing place
where God can repair the damage done
by the noise and pressure of the world.**

There is a meeting place as close as our closet door—a time and place where we can meet with God and hear His thoughts and He can hear ours; a time for the two of us when He can have our full attention and we can have His.

Solitude is where we are least alone and where our deepest loneliness can be relieved. It's a healing place where God can repair the damage done by the noise and pressure of the world. "The more you visit it," Thomas á Kempis said, "the more you will want to return."

"I will awaken the dawn," said David (Ps. 57:8). There's something to be said for meeting God before our busy days begin and our schedules begin to tyrannize us, though we must not understand this in some legalistic way to mean we have to get up before the sun to merit a meeting with God. For many, morning is the most opportune time; for others, it's more of an opportunity for the devil. There are times when it not only seems easier to meet with God, it is easier. It's something you have to work out with your body. The main thing is eagerness to meet Him. The advantage of doing so early is that we hear His thoughts before others invade our minds.

> **"Stay in that secret place till the surrounding noises begin to fade out of your heart, till a sense of God's presence has enveloped you. Listen for His inward voice till you learn to recognize it." —A. W. Tozer**

The first step is to find a Bible, a quiet place, and an uninterrupted period of time. Sit quietly and remind yourself that you're in the presence of God. He is there with you, eager to meet with you. "Stay in that secret place," A. W. Tozer said, "till the surrounding noises begin to fade out of your heart, till a sense of God's presence has enveloped you. Listen for His inward voice till you learn to recognize it."

Rest And Renewal; Taking Time Alone With God

Psalm 23:2—"He makes me to lie down in green pastures; He leads me beside the still waters."

Objective:
To know the Shepherd's rest by spending time in His presence.

Bible Memorization:
Psalm 23:2

Read:
"The Rest And Renewal Of The Shepherd" &
"Taking Time Alone With God"
pp.24-29

Warming Up
What person would you be most uncomfortable to be alone with? With whom would you most desire to spend time alone? Why?

Thinking Through
What does G. K. Chesterton mean when he suggests that the whole Bible is about the "loneliness of God" (p. 25). Do you think Chesterton is being irreverent or presumptuous, or is he presenting a profound biblical truth? Why?

In his confession on page 26, Malcolm Muggeridge mentions four inadequate responses to spiritual hunger. What are they? Which ones have you experienced? Do you share Muggeridge's conclusion?

On page 29, Tozer encourages us to stay in our "secret place." What is he referring to? Why should we spend time there? Where is your personal "secret place"?

Digging In
Key Text: Psalm 23:2
What idea was the psalmist portraying when he described sheep lying down?

How does the shepherd "lead" his sheep to "green pastures" and "quiet waters"? What condition does the shepherd have to create before his flock will "lie down"?

What is the reality behind the "green pastures" and "quiet waters" metaphors?

Going Further
Refer
Psalm 42:1-2 shows us another picture of being renewed by calming waters. What spiritual reality is represented in this picture of a deer drinking at a stream? What are the spiritual conditions that motivated the psalmist to want to meet with his God?

Reflect
Are you ever afraid to be alone with God? Why? In what way can it be a fearful thing to spend time alone with God?

Our lives often seem restless. What must occur before we can experience the peace we read about in this lesson? How can the picture of the shepherd leading us to green pastures and still waters strengthen us in the stressful times of life?

"He makes me to lie down in green pastures; He leads me beside the still waters."
Psalm 23:2

---

¹"As the deer pants for the water brooks, so pants my soul for You, O God. ²My soul thirsts for God, for the living God. When shall I come and appear before God?"
Psalm 42:1-2

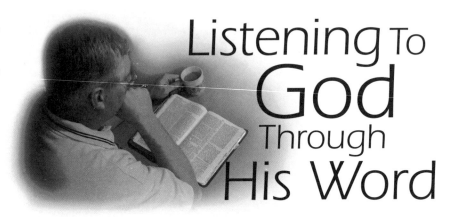

Listening To God Through His Word

Until we take time to be quiet, we'll not hear God. God cannot be heard in noise and restlessness; only in silence. He will speak to us if we will give Him a chance, if we will listen, if we will be quiet. "Be still," the psalmist wrote, "and know that I am God" (Ps. 46:10).

"Listen, listen to Me," God pleads, "and eat what is good, and your soul will delight in the richest of fare. Give ear and come to Me; hear Me, that your soul may live" (Isa. 55:2-3).

Listen to Him. There's no other way to take Him in. "When Your words came, I ate them" said Jeremiah (Jer. 15:16). Sit at His feet and let Him feed you. That's the "better" place to be (Lk. 10:38-42).

The problem with many of us is that though we read God's Word, we're not feeding on God. We're more intent on mastering the text—finding out its precise meaning, gathering theories and theologies—so we can talk more intelligently *about* God. The main purpose of reading the Bible, however, is not to accumulate data about Him, but to "come to Him," to encounter Him as our living God.

Jesus said to the best-read Bible students of His day, "You diligently study the Scriptures because you think that by them you possess eternal life. These are the Scriptures that testify about Me" (Jn. 5:39).

The scholars read the Bible, but they didn't listen to God; they "never heard His voice" (Jn. 5:37). We should do more than read words; we should seek the Word exposed in the words. We want to move beyond information to seeing God and being informed and shaped by His truth. There's a passing exhilaration—the "joy of discovery"—in acquiring knowledge about the Bible, but there's no life in it. The Bible is not an end in itself, but a stimulus to our interaction with God.

**The Bible is not an end in itself,
but a stimulus to our interaction with God.**

Start with a conscious desire to engage Him in a personal way. Select a portion of Scripture—a verse, a paragraph, a chapter—and read it over and over. Think of Him as present and speaking to you, disclosing His mind and emotions and will. God is articulate. He speaks to us through His Word. Meditate on His words until His thoughts begin to take shape in your mind.

Thoughts is exactly the right word because that's precisely what the Bible is—"the mind of the Lord" (1 Cor. 2:16). When we read His Word, we are reading His mind—what He knows, what He feels, what He wants, what He enjoys, what He desires, what He loves, what He hates.

Take time to reflect on what He is saying. Think about each word. Give yourself time for prayerful contemplation until God's heart is revealed and your heart is exposed.

Jean-Pierre de Caussade wrote, "Read quietly, slowly, word for word to enter into the subject more with the heart than with the mind. From time to time make short pauses to allow these truths time to flow through all the recesses of the soul."

Listen carefully to the words that touch your emotions and meditate on His goodness. "Feed on His faithfulness" (Ps. 37:3 NKJV). Think about His kindness and those glimpses of His unfailing love that motivate you to love Him more (Ps. 48:9). Savor His words. "Taste and see that the Lord is good" (Ps. 34:8).

Mother Teresa said, "Spend one hour a day in adoration of the Lord and you'll be all right." She might say something different to you and me. So much depends on our temperament, our family and job demands, the state of our health, our age and level of maturity. At first 10 or 15 minutes may be all we can manage. Then perhaps we will be ready for an hour every day. It's not important how much time we spend at first. The important thing is to make a beginning. God's Spirit will let us know where to go from there.

Our reading should be toward relishing God and delighting in Him—"to gaze upon the beauty of the Lord," as David said (Ps. 27:4). When we approach God in that way, it inclines us to want more of Him. "I have tasted Thee," Augustine said, "and now I hunger for Thee."

There's no need to worry about texts that we don't understand. Some meanings will escape us. Everything difficult indicates something more than our hearts can yet embrace. As Jesus said to His disciples, "I have much more to say to you, more than you can now bear" (Jn. 16:12). There's much that we will never know, but some of the hard questions will be answered when we're ready for them.

God can never be understood through the intellect. Insight arises from purity of heart—from love, humility, and a desire to obey. It's the "pure in heart" who "will see God," Jesus said (Mt. 5:8). The more of God's truth we know and want to obey, the more we know.

George MacDonald wrote, "The words of the Lord are seeds sown in our hearts by the sower. They have to fall into our hearts to grow. Meditation and prayer must water them and obedience keep them in the light. Thus they will bear fruit for the Lord's gathering."

We shouldn't worry about our doubts either. How could God possibly reveal Himself in a way that would leave no room for doubt? Madeleine L'Engle said, "Those who believe they believe in God . . . without anguish of mind, without uncertainty, without doubt, and even at times without despair, believe only in the idea of God, not in God Himself."

Uncertainty is the name of the game. The best thing is to take our questionings and doubts directly to God, as David often did. His psalms are filled with discomfort and disagreement with God's ways. He fills page after page with confusion and disbelief. It's good to do so. God can handle our hesitancy.

Sometimes we're mentally dull or emotionally flat, weary, and tired. On such occasions it's worthless to try to make ourselves think more deeply or respond more intensely. If the value of our times alone with God depends on our emotional state, we will always be troubled. We should never worry about how we feel. Even when our minds are confused or our hearts are cold we can learn from our solitude. Don't try to make your heart love God. Just give it to Him.

If we're having a hard time with God, if we don't yet trust His heart, we should read the Gospels—Matthew, Mark, Luke, and John. There we hear what Jesus said and did and what was said about Him. There we see Him making visible the invisible God. When Philip, Jesus' disciple, asked to see God, Jesus replied, "Don't you know Me, Philip, even after I have been among you such a long time? Anyone who has seen Me has seen the Father. How can you say, 'Show us the Father'?" (Jn. 14:9).

One commentator has written, "Philip's request is the profound expression of deep hunger behind the whole religious quest, speaking for saints and mystics, thinkers, moralists, and men of faith of every age. 'He that hath seen Me hath seen the Father,' is Christ's staggering response. That is what the doctrine of Christ's divine Sonship really means, and why it matters. In His words we hear God speaking; in His deeds we see God at work; in His reproach we glimpse God's judgment; in His love we feel God's heart beating. If this be not true, we know nothing of God at all. If it be true—and we know it is—then Jesus is God manifest in the flesh, the unique, incomparable, only begotten Son of the Living God."

The main use of the Gospels is to help us see the character of God made real, personal, and understandable in Jesus. What we see Jesus doing—caring, suffering, weeping, calling, seeking—is what God is doing and has been doing all along. If you can't love God, try to see Him in Jesus. There He's revealed as One who has no limits to His love; One to whom we can come with all our doubts, disappointments, and misjudgments; One "whom we can approach without fear and to whom we can submit ourselves without despair" (Blaise Pascal). In the Gospels we see that God is the only God worth having.

Listening To God Through His Word

Psalm 37:3—"Trust in the Lord, and do good; dwell in the land, and feed on His faithfulness."

Objective:
To experience the Shepherd's renewal by spending time in His Word.

Bible Memorization:
Psalm 37:3

Read:
"Listening To God Through His Word"
pp.32-35

Warming Up

Have you ever tried to have a serious conversation with a distracted and busy person or with someone in a hurry? How was it difficult? How did you feel about the lack of attention that person gave you?

Thinking Through

On page 32, we are warned of the danger of studying the Bible to master the text instead of feeding on God. How are these things different? Why is studying only to master the text potentially dangerous?

What did Augustine mean when he said, "I have tasted Thee, and now I hunger for Thee"? (p.34). How did these words express his hunger for worship and his delight in God Himself?

On page 35 we read, "The main use of the Gospels is to help us see the character of God made real, personal, and understandable in Jesus." How did Jesus reveal different aspects of God's character?

Digging In
Key Text: Luke 10:38-42

Both Mary and Martha desired to please the Lord, but they went about it in different ways. What are the positive and negative elements in both approaches?

What did Jesus mean when He said, "One thing is needed"? (v.42). Why do you think the Lord did not say that Martha's choice was wrong, only that Mary's was "good" (v.42). In what ways was Mary's choice good?

What does this passage teach about the need for balance between our need to be busy for the Lord and our need for intimacy with the Lord?

Going Further
Refer
According to Psalm 19:7-8, what are four characteristics of the Word of God and four ways it benefits us?

Reflect
We live in a world where quietness is rare. Why is quietness often uncomfortable for us? What do we sometimes do to avoid the discomfort of quiet?

Do you identify more with Martha or Mary? If Martha, how can quiet times in God's Word help you to be more effective in your practical service for the Lord?

38 "Now it happened as they went that He entered a certain village; and a certain woman named Martha welcomed Him into her house. 39 And she had a sister called Mary, who also sat at Jesus' feet and heard His word. 40 But Martha was distracted with much serving, and she approached Him and said, 'Lord, do You not care that my sister has left me to serve alone? Therefore tell her to help me.' 41 And Jesus answered and said to her, 'Martha, Martha, you are worried and troubled about many things. 42 But one thing is needed, and Mary has chosen that good part, which will not be taken away from her.'"
Luke 10:38-42

7 The law of the Lord is perfect, converting the soul; the testimony of the Lord is sure, making wise the simple; 8 the statutes of the Lord are right, rejoicing the heart; the commandment of the Lord is pure, enlightening the eyes."
Psalm 19:7-8

Responding To God In Prayer

As we listen to God, we should answer. This is prayer—our response to the revelation and unfolding of God's heart. "My God, Thy creature answers Thee," said the French poet, Alfred de Musset. Prayer, understood in that way, is an extension of our visits with God rather than something tacked on.

Our meetings with God are like a polite conversation with a friend. They're not monologues in which one person does all the talking and the other does all the listening, but dialogues in which we listen thoughtfully to one another's self-disclosure and then respond.

One of my colleagues describes the process this way: If we're reading a note from a loved one in which we're praised, loved, appreciated, counseled, corrected, and helped in various ways and that individual is present in the room while we read, it's only right that we should express thanks, reciprocate love, ask questions, and in other ways react to the message. It would be rude to do otherwise. This is prayer.

Around 1370, a book was published with the title *The Cloud Of Unknowing*. It's thought that the author was a spiritual director in a monastery, but we don't know his name. Much of what he wrote is hard to understand, but when it comes to prayer he was profoundly simple.

God, he said, can be known, even through "the cloud of unknowing" by responding to Him with "just a little word . . . the shorter it is the better." His book is a textbook of succinct and simple prayer:

It is good to think of Your kindness, O God, and to love You and praise You for that. Yet it is far better to think upon Your simple being, and to love You and praise You for Yourself. Lord, I covet You and seek You and nothing but You. My God, You are all I need, and more; whoever has You needs nothing else in this life.

If you don't know where to start, pray David's psalms. David's life was characterized by prayer. In Psalm 109:4 David wrote, "In return for my friendship they accuse me, but I am a man of prayer." The translators supplied "a man of," but the text reads simply, "but I am prayer." Prayer was the essence of David's life and his genius, as it is ours. We have this access to God, this intimacy with Him, this opportunity to receive all that the heart of God has stored up for us. It is the means by which we receive God's gifts, the means by which everything is done. David teaches us to pray.

Prayer is an extension of our visits with God rather than something tacked on.

Prayer is worship. Our praying should be full of adoration, affection, and fondness for God that He is who He is, that He created us in order to have someone on whom He could shower His love, that He stretched out His arms on the cross, and that He intends, in the fullest sense, to make whole men and women out of us. In worship, as the old word *worth-ship* implies, we declare what we value the most. It is one of the best ways in the world to love God.

Prayer is the highest expression of our dependence on God. It is asking for what we want. We can ask for anything—even the most difficult things. "Do not be anxious about anything, but in everything, by prayer and petition, with thanksgiving, present your requests to God" (Phil. 4:6). Anything large enough to occupy our minds is large enough to hang a prayer on.

Prayer, however, by its nature is requesting. It is not insisting or clamoring. We can make no demands of God or deals with Him. Furthermore, we're coming to a friend. Friends don't make demands. They ask and then wait. We wait with patience and submission until God gives us what we request—or something more.

David wrote, "I have stilled and quieted my soul; like a weaned child with its mother, like a weaned child is my soul within me" (Ps. 131:2). David was in exile, waiting for God, learning not to worry himself with God's delays and other mysterious ways. No longer restless and craving, he waited for God to answer in His own time and in His own way. He is able to do far more than anything we can ask or imagine, but He must do it in His time and in His way. We ask in our time and in our way; God answers in His.

Prayer is asking for understanding. It is the means by which we comprehend what God is saying to us in His Word. The process by which we gain awareness of His mind is not natural, but supernatural. Spiritual things are discerned spiritually (1 Cor. 2:6-16). There is truth that can never be grasped by the human intellect. It cannot be discovered; it must be disclosed. Certainly we can understand the facts in the Bible apart from God's help, but we can never plumb its depths, never fully appreciate "what God has prepared for those who love Him" (v.9). We must pray and wait for truth to come honestly into our minds.

Prayer moves what we know from our heads to our hearts.

Prayer moves what we know from our heads to our hearts. It's our hedge against hypocrisy, the way by which we begin to ring true. Our perceptions of truth are always ahead of our condition. Prayer brings us more into conformity. It bridges the gap between what we know and what we are.

Prayer focuses and unites our fragmented hearts. We have a thousand necessities. It's impossible for us to purify them and simplify them and integrate them into one. David prayed, "Give me an undivided heart" (Ps. 86:11). He wanted to love God with his whole heart, but he couldn't sustain the effort. Other interests and affections pulled him and divided him, so he asked God to guard his heart and unite its affections into one.

The prophet Isaiah wrote, "He wakens me morning by morning, wakens my ear to listen like one being taught. The Sovereign Lord has opened my ears, and I have not been rebellious; I have not drawn back" (Isa. 50:4-5). Centering on

God each morning should be done as though it had never been done before. In that quiet place He comforts us, He instructs us, He listens to us, He prepares our hearts and strengthens us for the day. There we learn to love Him and worship Him again. We esteem His words and defer to Him once more. We get His fresh perspective on the problems and possibilities of our day.

Then we should take His presence with us all through the day—journeying, pausing, waiting, listening, recalling what He said to us in the morning. He is our teacher, our philosopher, our friend; our gentlest, kindest, and most interesting companion.

He is with us wherever we go. He is in the commonplace, whether we know it or not. "Surely the Lord is in this place," Jacob said of a most unlikely location, "and I was not aware of it" (Gen. 28:16). We may not realize that He is close by. We may feel lonely and sad and desolate. Our day may seem bleak and dreary without a visible ray of hope, yet He is present.

God has said, "Never will I leave you; never will I forsake you."
So we say with confidence, "The Lord is my helper; I will not be afraid"
(Heb. 13:5-6).

The clamor of this visible and audible world is so persistent and God's quiet voice sometimes is so faint that we forget that He is near. But not to worry: He cannot forget us.

In God's presence there is satisfaction. His lush meadows are boundless. His still water runs deep. "There," I say to myself, "[I] will lie down in good grazing land, and there [I] will feed in a rich pasture" (Ezek. 34:14).

STUDY
NO. **6**

Responding To God In Prayer

Philippians 4:6—"Be anxious for nothing, but in everything by prayer and supplication, with thanksgiving, let your requests be made known to God."

Objective:
To enjoy the Shepherd's presence as we learn to go to Him in prayer.

Bible Memorization:
Philippians 4:6

Read:
"Responding To God In Prayer" pp.38-41

Warming Up
What frustrates you about your prayer-life? Why? What encourages you in your prayer-life? Why? How do those frustrations and encouragements affect your desire to pray?

Thinking Through
On page 39 it says that "prayer is worship." If so, what elements should always be a part of your prayer-time? Why are these elements so important?

What are the implications of the statement, "Prayer is the highest expression of our dependence on God"? (p.39). How is this seen in your prayers, and how does it define the difference between requesting and insisting? (p.39).

According to page 40, why is it so important that you pray with the psalmist, "Give me an undivided heart"? (Ps. 86:11). How can the distractions and necessities of life undermine your prayers? In what ways have you experienced this?

Digging In
Key Text: Philippians 4:6-7
How are anxiety and prayer powerful yet opposing forces in the Christian experience?

What do you tend to do with your worries? Is prayer your first option, or your last? Does prayer help to relieve your anxiety and stress? If so, how?

What is the "peace of God" that Paul mentions in verse 7? What does Paul mean when he says that this peace is one that "surpasses all understanding" and "will guard your hearts and minds through Christ Jesus"?

Going Further
Refer
Jesus is described as being motivated by compassion for those who are suffering. See if you can identify at least five places in the Gospels where this occurs. What does this tell you about praying for God's comfort when you are plagued by anxiety?

Reflect
If prayer is so important, why don't we devote more time and effort to it? What changes do you need to make if you are to become a person of prayer?

How has this study helped you trust the Shepherd in the hardships of life? What life principles can you apply on a daily basis, not only in your own experience but also in your ministry to others who are hurting?

[6]"Be anxious for nothing, but in everything by prayer and supplication, with thanksgiving, let your requests be made known to God;
[7]and the peace of God, which surpasses all understanding, will guard your hearts and minds through Christ Jesus."
Philippians 4:6-7

Discovery Series Bible Study Leader's And User's Guide

Statement Of Purpose

The *Discovery Series Bible Study* (DSBS) series provides assistance to pastors and leaders in discipling and teaching Christians through the use of RBC Ministries *Discovery Series* booklets. The DSBS series uses the inductive Bible-study method to help Christians understand the Bible more clearly.

Study Helps

Listed at the beginning of each study are the key verse, objective, and memorization verses. These will act as the compass and map for each study.

Some key Bible passages are printed out fully. This will help the students to focus on these passages and to examine and compare the Bible texts more easily—leading to a better understanding of their meanings. Serious students are encouraged to open their own Bible to examine the other Scriptures as well.

How To Use DSBS (for individuals and small groups)

Individuals—Personal Study
- Read the designated pages of the book.
- Carefully consider and answer all the questions.

Small Groups—Bible-Study Discussion
- To maximize the value of the time spent together, each member should do the lesson work prior to the group meeting.
- Recommended discussion time: 45–55 minutes.
- Engage the group in a discussion of the questions, seeking full participation from each of the members.

Overview Of Lessons

The DSBS format incorporates a "layered" approach to Bible study that includes four segments. These segments form a series of perspectives that become increasingly more personalized and focused. These segments are:

Warming Up. In this section, a general interest question is used to begin the discussion (in small groups) or "to get the juices flowing" (in personal study). It is intended to begin the process of interaction at the broadest, most general level.

Thinking Through. Here, the student or group is invited to interact with the *Discovery Series* material that has been read. In considering the information and implications of the booklet, these questions help to drive home the critical concepts of that portion of the booklet.

Digging In. Moving away from the *Discovery Series* material, this section isolates a key biblical text from the manuscript and engages the student or group in a brief inductive study of that passage of Scripture. This brings the authority of the Bible into the forefront of the study as we consider its message to our hearts and lives.

Going Further. This final segment contains two parts. In Refer, the student or group has the opportunity to test the ideas of the lesson against the rest of the Bible by cross-referencing the text with other verses. In Reflect, the student or group is challenged to personally apply the lesson by making a practical response to what has been learned.

Pulpit Sermon Series (for pastors and church leaders)

Although the *Discovery Series Bible Study* is primarily for personal and group study, pastors may want to use this material as the foundation for a series of messages on this important issue. The suggested topics and their corresponding texts are as follows:

Sermon No.	Topic	Text
1	David And The Shepherd Metaphor	Ps. 23:1
2	Others Who Used The Shepherd Metaphor	Ezek. 34:11-16
3	The Shepherd Metaphor To Describe Jesus	Jn. 10:11-16
4	Taking Time Alone With God	Ps. 23:2
5	Listening To God Through His Word	Lk. 10:38-42
6	Responding To God In Prayer	Phil. 4:6-7

Final Thoughts

The DSBS will provide an opportunity for growth and ministry. To internalize the spiritual truths of each study in a variety of environments, the material is arranged to allow for flexibility in the application of the truths discussed.

Whether DSBS is used in small-group Bible studies, adult Sunday school classes, adult Bible fellowships, men's and women's study groups, or church-wide applications, the key to the strength of the discussion will be found in the preparation of each participant. Likewise, the effectiveness of personal and pastoral use of this material will be directly related to the time committed to using this resource.

As you use, teach, or study this material, may you "grow in the grace and knowledge of our Lord and Savior Jesus Christ" (2 Pet. 3:18).

OUR DAILY BREAD

Delivered right to your home!

What could be better than getting *Our Daily Bread?* How about having it delivered directly to your home?

You'll also have the opportunity to receive special offers or Bible-study booklets. And you'll get articles written on timely topics we all face, such as forgiveness and anger.

To order your copy of *Our Daily Bread,* write to us at:

USA: PO Box 2222, Grand Rapids, MI 49501-2222
CANADA: Box 1622, Windsor, ON N9A 6Z7

RBC Web site: www.odb.org/guide

RBC Ministries
RADIO BIBLE CLASS ~ FOUNDED 1938